A Little

Book of

Mourning

A Little Book of

Mourning

By Katherine Lench Meyering

© 2024 Katherine Lench Meyering,
All Rights Reserved

ISBN 978-1-7360036-1-9

For Alex

Under the water. Under the sky.
Much deeper than I dare to fly.
The current takes me far away
from time and sound and light.

A LITTLE BOOK OF MOURNING

I woke up today and said, "This is it. This is the day I finish the book. I close the chapter. I turn the page. I will send it out into the world."

It's time to share.

And then I thought, "It's never over."
This agony can't end. It's the only thing I can be sure of. But I've come to understand that though the grief won't end, it will change. It will soften. It will become part of my story. It will become part of my history. It will not dominate my every thought. It will not crush my spirit. That is not to say that I can't be returned to square one by a sound, smell, thought, encounter or remembrance.

It is to say that I will survive. We will survive.

I have learned that I am not alone, and that there are too many others going through the same process. I hope this helps someone.

I know it helped me.

Katherine Lench Meyering

The pain I gained transported me to freedom underneath the sun

It starts and ends with love

~ Katherine Lench Meyering
September 17, 2024

A Little Book of Mourning
SUKIYAKI

Tonight, I am afraid that if I start crying, I'll never stop.

Just before my father died, we gathered in his room for that rare day just before the end. He rallied and was happy. We served him a big gin martini and brought him his favorite caviar and chopped egg sandwiches. We were all singing the old songs; the ones we knew in English, German, Yiddish, French and Japanese.

My father spoke multiple languages. In his sixties, he started studying Japanese. He said he was actually too old to start a new language, so he gave his Japanese dictionary to Alex. That language became Alex's passion. She eventually moved to Japan and taught English to Japanese children.

Listening to the two of them sing this seemingly happy -- yet sad and reflective -- song about being alone and remembering the seasons, I admired their strength and deep love for one another.

Tonight, I am thinking of that song, "Sukiyaki." Of the sad and haunting message it evoked.

Katherine Lench Meyering

My friend, Camille, said it best, "For some people, life is a struggle. There is a darkness that lives in some hearts which no light can overcome. We can never truly know what someone else is going through. All we can do is offer our love and support. Last night the darkness came for Alex and she could not push it away. She will always be with us. In our memories, in her songs, in her words and in her art."

Alexandra Mitsch-Meyering

August 11, 1989 - August 24, 2021

A Little Book of Mourning

౹౸౸

INNISFREE

August 2021

"The Lake Isle of Innisfree," William Butler Yeats

I will arise and go now, and go to Innisfree,
And a small cabin build there, of clay
       and wattles made;
Nine bean-rows will I have there,
       a hive for the honey-bee,
And live alone in the bee-loud glade.

And I shall have some peace there,
       for peace comes dropping slow,
Dropping from the veils of the morning
       to where the cricket sings;
There midnight's all a glimmer, and noon
       a purple glow,
And evening full of the linnet's wings.

I will arise and go now, for always night and day
I hear lake water lapping with low sounds
       by the shore;
While I stand on the roadway, or on
       the pavements grey,
I hear it in the deep heart's core.

This was one of Alex's favorite poems.

Katherine Lench Meyering

Our family loves words, poetry, songs, theater, music, and food.

My mother, Judy, would read to me and my brother Dan, and then later to Alex and her brother Max, and cousins Raleigh and Dylan. My mother loved old legends and Chaucer and intellectual pursuits. Many an evening we would sit around her bounteous dinner table and recite our favorite poems, and sing our favorite songs.

It was a rare and fine time, and each of us would have their own special contribution to the entertainment -- the ones we performed best.

When I was younger, I couldn't wait for my turn to shine. I would hear the sound and meter of the other poems but would very rarely take in their meaning.

My mother and Alex were kindred spirits and spent their lives delving into the complexities of each word. To me, I liked the sound.

Tonight, as I grieve Alex's loss, and sleep will not come, I thought I'd take out her favorite poem and read it and delve into the complexities. But I find that, to me, it is simple and lovely and lyrical. And I see that between my mother, Alex, and me it can be seen and heard and savored any way you want.

When it was finally Alex's turn to recite, she would have a rapturous look on her face, and she would glow with her love of this poem. I loved that look on her face, and loved the sound of her voice, and respected her deeper understanding of it.

I hope my Alex has found her bee-loud glade. I hope she finds some peace there. And I wish I could hear her recite it one more time.

୧୨

NATIONAL DAUGHTERS DAY
September 25, 2021

On National Daughters Day, I am reminded of a time when Alex and I switched roles. She became the mother and I the daughter.

We were driving to Cambria, just the two of us. We would periodically have a mother-daughter weekend in her favorite town. We'd go wine tasting, go antique shopping, visit the graveyard and pay our respects, go to Linn's bakery and the Sow's Ear, sleep late and have fun.

On this particular time, we left early in the morning to beat the traffic and heat. We left at about 5:00 a.m. and it was still dark. There was fog on the Grapevine and it came upon us suddenly. I was blinded and couldn't see anything.

Anyone who knows me knows I'm not a great driver. I was terrified. I could not see. I began to panic and admitted to Alex that this was my worst nightmare. I was driving blind.

Then came her voice: calm, adult, practical. Saying, "You're ok. Just breathe. Let's slow down. Can you get to the right lane?"

My voice sounded like who I was, a frightened child. "I can't see. I can't do this. We could get hurt."

Katherine Lench Meyering

"No, we have this. We can do this. You're ok. See you're doing so well."

After what seemed to be forever, the fog lifted a bit. We got through it. With her voice, kindness, calm steady belief we were safe. She guided me out of the blindness.

We got to Cambria and had a wonderful time.

Thank you, Alex.

Happy National Daughters Day.

I miss you.

A Little Book of Mourning

TELLING THE BEES

My girlfriend, Marjorie Poe, sent me an article a couple of days after Alex passed about an old tradition on English and French farms where the mistress of the house was supposed to inform their hives of bees about births and deaths in the family. If they didn't tell the bees, terrible things would happen on the farm. The cows would run dry, the fields would not produce, etc.

Just after Alex passed, I went outside because Marjorie said, "Go tell the bees." I couldn't find any bees, so I told a moth. I asked him to tell a bee. Then the next day, I found a bee and shared the news!

Katherine Lench Meyering

"Fly Little Bee"
(lyrics by Katherine Lench Meyering, music by Marjorie Poe)

Fly little bee tell all you know
Our girl is gone.
She left us cold in the dark of night.
She's gone, gone, gone.

Tell all the birds the air and trees
Our girl is gone.
She left us here in the dark and cold.
She's gone, gone, gone.

The spiders need to spin it.
The fox must cry aloud.
Oh bees please tell the linnet.
That bird could tell a cloud.

Fly little bee tell all you know
Our girl is with you now.
We're waiting here in the light of day,
Light of day.
She's gone, gone, gone.

A Little Book of Mourning

WHAT DO I DO WITH THE JEWELRY?
October 2021

It's been two months, one day and a few minutes since I heard the news that would change my life forever. My beautiful, complicated, fascinating, cursed with incurable depression, daughter took her life. She couldn't take it one more second, and with a quick jump from a chair, shattered the lives of all who knew her. That news rippled out to the friends of friends of friends.

Her friends, fans, and followers on Facebook, Instagram, Twitter, and various groups involved with her novels and video game pursuits, gave a collective sob that I hear in the dead of night or in the busiest parts of my day. Every corner of my house, and every corner of our neighborhood, reminds me of her. There is not a store or restaurant or hike that doesn't scream her name. I seem to remember everything all at once. Sleep, when it comes, is full of dreams and signs and images that haunt me more than any ghost could.

I had to take down the pictures. I had to start to prepare a bag for Goodwill. I had to start the slow process of dimming her light in order to survive. It doesn't make me feel much better but, it is necessary. And I'm told, with time, the wound will never heal but the scar won't hurt as much. Strangely, the scar from her C-section 32 years ago still hurts. I know my time is limited. I'll be sixty-five in a month. So, what to do with the rest of my life? What projects should I throw myself into? Do I start a foundation? Do I dedicate my life to getting her last unpublished novel published? Do I figure out what to do with her amazing art work? Her pug caricatures?

And what do I do with the jewelry? I have to rewrite my will. I have to leave what is most

A Little Book of Mourning

precious to me to someone. But who will understand the significance of my great-aunt's pearls, or of the brooch with the pink and green stones I wore for my wedding which belonged to my great-grandmother? Who will care about the 100-year-old hand mirror my grandmother proudly passed down to her daughter who gave it to me? And what about the platinum and pearl chain that belonged to the great actress who gave it to my speech professor who gave it to me? What about my engagement ring, with the five European cut diamonds, and my mother's beloved yellow pearl necklace with the tiny blue crystal beads? What do I possibly do with the cut crystal necklace my aunt gave to me which my beautiful, complicated, gone forever daughter wore to her prom?

I have taken down most of the pictures and I have located most of the jewelry, including the ladies pocket watch that my grandfather gave to my grandmother; which was her pride and joy. I have sorted the many earrings and bits of silver and gold and my mother's wedding ring and my father's wedding ring and my own. Who will understand?

She would have. She didn't even wear much jewelry. But she knew the history and she cared.

I remember she came to see me playing the lead in a musical when she was ten or eleven. She came backstage and declared to me and the room, "Oh Mama, you're so sparkly!" Of all the compliments she gave me, and there were many, that is the one that sticks. I like bling. I've been a performer all my life and I have loads of sparkly necklaces and bracelets. They were all too gaudy for her. The jewels that were given to her, she usually made displays of. She constructed little shrines of gems and chains.

A Little Book of Mourning

When I started to help clear her room with her husband, and mother and father-in-law, we went through her jewelry boxes and found the first ruby ring her father and I had given her for her for her thirteenth birthday. We found many strange earrings -- some of which had flowers and teapots and teacups and bird cages on them. She had a steampunk kind of taste. Lots of Lolita dresses and cameos. We found many of the tree-of-life necklaces my friend had made for her, and a clump of chains to be untangled. But we could not find the charm bracelet her dear mother-in-law had given her. Her mother-in-law had once intended to keep adding charms to that bracelet and it was nowhere to be found.

We searched for a long time and were just about to look through purses and pockets when we took a break. After lunch and before leaving, I decided to give it one more try. Her mother-in-law was with me. I went into the center of her room and asked aloud saying,

Katherine Lench Meyering

"Okay, where is it?" In a second, I knew. The knowledge dropped into my head. I walked over to a bookcase and behind a doll/music box that played "Mary Had a Little Lamb" was the bracelet. We all had goose bumps.

It was one of many moments that makes me feel she is with me. Guiding me. Helping me through this waking nightmare. She is probably telling me who should get which piece of jewelry. But I haven't asked. Maybe it's time to stand in the middle of the room and ask, "What do I do with the jewelry?"

A Little Book of Mourning

I HAD TO GIVE UP MY FEAR OF FLYING
November 13, 2021

I used to be terrified of flying. I couldn't comprehend what forces kept such huge flying machines in the air. To be honest, I never liked the feeling of motion, got dizzy on fast theme park rides, was afraid of heights and not crazy about boats or even going above the speed limit in a car. While some people thrive on the feeling they get in the pits of their stomachs when turbulence hits, I would look frantically around for the barf bag.

I used to avoid flying at almost all costs, but when my mother broke her ankle horribly while on a trip to England with my father, I was forced to fly and help them return to California. They were older and flew me over for assistance and moral support. I remember receiving my itinerary so quickly that I didn't have time to worry about the ten-hour flight.

Katherine Lench Meyering

But on the morning of my departure, I started to panic. My breath came in starts and fits. My stomach tied itself in knots and threatened to explode. My palms were dripping and I doubted I could withstand the marathon day about to unfold. I was traveling alone and had always been very sensitive to any kind of medicine. Even aspirin made me ill. So, I was going to fly cold turkey.

I got to my seat, stowed my carry on, buckled my seatbelt, gripped the seat arms, and closed my eyes, praying to whichever God was listening. Just before takeoff, the man who was seated next to me must have seen my pale face and smiled at me. We struck up one of those conversations that happen only on airplanes. I find I'll tell a complete stranger some of my deepest secrets, knowing I'll never see them again. He asked what I did for a living and I divulged that I had been a secretary who had worked for the branch of the Walt Disney Company that designed

A Little Book of Mourning

Disneylands -- Walt Disney Imagineering. And before that, I was an actress and singer who pursued my dreams of working on Broadway. He listened attentively and then told me that he was a hypnotist. He was flying to London to help some professional golfers engage their subconsciouses in order to hit golf balls farther and more accurately.

Then, a bell rang in my ears and I asked him how his techniques worked on fear of flying? He smiled a secret grin and said, "It's one of my specialties!" He saw my obvious distress and asked if he could be of service. He asked me to describe the worst possible thing that could happen on this flight. I said, "The plane could crash and we would all perish." He told me to close my eyes and envision the crash. He told me not to leave out any of the horrifying details. He then said, "Now run the crash in your mind at high speed as if it were a movie." Then he instructed me to rewind the movie and show it to myself backwards --

from the crash to me sitting comfortably in my seat. Then he said for me to run it forward in my mind, but this time in slow motion. Then he directed me to run it forward, but this time to add funny circus clown music to what I saw. Next, he asked me where my fear presented in my body. I told him that I felt it in my stomach. "And which direction is the fear traveling in?" he queried. I said it was moving clockwise. He told me to reverse the direction by placing my hand near my tummy and to make a counterclockwise motion. Then he asked where my fear was located at the moment. I pointed to my left shoulder. He reached over, made a grasping motion at my shoulder, and threw my "fear" away in a quick gesture. He looked me deep in my eyes, proclaiming, "Now it's gone!"

And just like that, it was gone. I was distracted by all the mental tasks and somehow, I wasn't afraid anymore. It was miraculous. I settled down, watched a few movies, ate the airplane cuisine and arrived to save the day.

I don't even know his name but he appeared, like an angel and cured me.

Whenever I flew, with the exception of my last two flights, I would go through the same mental paces he taught me and would settle back and enjoy the ride. I've even comforted nervous flyers squeezed into seats next to me. I also added an additional step in my "preparation for flight" routine. I imagined my mother's voice. On the first airplane ride I ever took, she was by my side. I remember her telling me it was like riding in a big bus. She told me there would be a loud noise, then a little bump and we'd be in the air. She said, "See, wasn't that fun?" And because she was my mom and she was magic, I agreed.

Katherine Lench Meyering

But recently, in the wake of an unspeakable tragedy, my fear of flying tried to make a comeback. On August 24th of this year, my daughter took her life. She died, as I'm learning from others who have experienced this kind of loss, from an incurable depression. She tried in vain for 32 years to keep her demons at bay, but on that fateful

A Little Book of Mourning

Tuesday night the demons came for her and won the war.

What was hard to comprehend was that she seemed to be getting better. I also understand that many parents of children who die from suicide say the same thing. We were blindsided by her. We were left reeling then, and still are.

At the end of May, I had a surgery on my knee. My husband was out of town and I was helpless for a few days. My daughter came to stay with me and nursed me. She gave me her time selflessly for about a week. She had just completed her master's degree and was unwinding from the enormous pressures of tests, papers, and applying and being accepted into a doctoral program. But she sprang into action and, in a role reversal, became a parent to me.

Katherine Lench Meyering

She brought food, watched all six seasons of *Schitt's Creek* with me and we talked and laughed like mother and daughter and friends and confidants. It was the kind of relationship I had always yearned to have with her, but her profound angst, tendencies to drink too much, and her cavalier attitude toward spending money like water got in the way. We always had a deep love for one another, but there were times when our liking of each other was strained.

But I will always remember and cherish that week. If I had known that it would be the last time we would be together like that, I would have stayed up all night every night. I would have told and retold my favorite stories to her. I would have listened to her beautiful voice speaking to me, singing to me, telling me jokes. I would have told her in words how much I loved and admired her for her wit, intelligence, beauty, love of animals, writing skills, piano playing, fine art, and just the way she laughed. I would have told her that even in her rages and dark times she was precious to me. I hope she understood. I will never know for sure.

Ten days after my surgery, my daughter and her husband drove me to the airport to fly and meet my husband. I had to wear compression leg machines to prevent blood clots, and had to be taken in a wheelchair through the airport. Not only was I worrying about the actual flight, I was worried about getting a deep vein thrombosis. As I waited to board at 6:00 a.m., I started to begin my mental "preparation for flight" routine, but being carted around like a piece of luggage in my wheelchair took me out of sequence. Before I knew it, we were airborne. The machines on my legs were squeezing me and my breathing became shallow. Try as I would, I couldn't calm myself down. So, I used a secret weapon I had learned from my many nights of insomnia. I began to count backwards from

Katherine Lench Meyering

forty-nine to zero. Then I tried singing "Twinkle, Twinkle, Little Star" in my mind backwards. Deep breathing followed and by sheer force of will I managed to get through the flight. I worried that my hypnotic magic might have deserted me.

But since the end of August my world has been irrevocably altered. I've had to fly again recently, but I'm a different person. I had to give up my fear of flying along with getting worked up or upset about having my blood drawn or getting into an automobile accident. I've had to give up fretting because one of the worst things that could happen to a person happened to me. I lost my first-born child. I lost her comfort, her companionship, watching her grow older, bragging about her accomplishments, and the sound of her voice. I still expect to see her walking up to our front door, asking, "What's for dinner and where's the wine?"

A Little Book of Mourning

As I boarded my last flight, I greeted the stewardess and buckled myself in. I didn't look at the card telling me where the exits were. I noticed the lady next to me as she gripped the arms of her seat. The captain came on apologizing -- saying we would be flying through lots of weather this morning. He said we were in for a bumpy ride. The lady next to me began to frantically look for a Xanax in her carry on. I told her it would be all right. And it was indeed a bumpy ride. And I didn't mind in the slightest when the plane bobbed up and down. I just went with

the buffeting feeling. I said hello to my stomach and heard my mother's voice say, "See, wasn't that fun?"

Katherine Lench Meyering

A Little Book of Mourning

☙❧

THE SUN AND THE RIVER

November 15, 2021

A story I wrote to get through the day.

It was winter on Earth and the Sun was worried that her presence would ruin the frozen, glittery landscape she saw when she rose one early December morning. She was pleased that her rays splashed pink and melon colors over the river and its banks causing the water beneath to heat ever so slightly. She was flattered when she saw herself reflected in the frozen icicles and delicately frosted trees that stood like powdered statues waiting patiently for something to happen. She knew that she couldn't stay too long gazing at her reflected glory, for she saw that already there was mist rising from the river and she could spoil this pristine moment.

It wasn't like her to worry about anything much but getting up early and going to bed each night. It took a great deal of energy to exist at all, so she rarely looked down at the earth. But that morning was like no other she could remember. That morning, she lingered, and for a thing made of gas and fire, gasped at the sparkling beauty that lay quiet and majestic beneath her.

As the Sun was pondering a way to capture this moment and keep it forever untouched, a little white fox crawled out from under a pine tree and made its way to the river to freshen up and get a drink. The fox was shivering, as it was very cold, and looked around to see if any hunters or dogs were nearby. The white furry creature slunk toward the water cautiously. The Sun saw the fox and in a split second shone her warm smile upon it. The white fox looked up and was transformed into a little girl with bright red hair, dressed from head to toe in white fur.

A Little Book of Mourning

The girl, who we shall call Hazel, was astonished to be so changed. But wrapped in her white fur dress, hat, cape and snow shoes, was warm as could be. Hazel laughed delightedly to see her breath floating in the air ahead of her. She turned around, took a step and fell down flat on her back. As she struggled to get up, she moved her new found arms and legs up and down. Scrambling to her feet, she looked at her impression in the snow and thought, "What an odd shape I have." Just then, an otter scurried up from the river and slipped and slid into the depression in the snow Hazel made. As he lay there panting from his exertions, the Sun smiled and a ray caught the otter and, in an instant, he became a little boy dressed in dark fur. He knew, magically, that his name was Phinneas. He stood up, brushed the snow from his furry coat, and laughed joyously to see Hazel.

He bowed low, and addressed her as if she were a princess. "How do you do, milady?" he said. "I couldn't help but see you standing on the shore." Hazel gave a polite nod to Phinneas and asked him to explain how he happened to become a boy right before her eyes. Phinneas had no idea and asked her the same question.

Before they had a chance to answer each others' questions, the Sun spoke in a warm and loving voice telling them both that they each had had the most beautiful fur the Sun had ever seen and that she wanted to reward them by turning them into the prince and princess of this wintry realm. All they had to do was to maintain the beauty and serenity of this morning and they would enjoy long and healthy lives. With that, the Sun said she must hurry away. She told them she had already stayed too long and was late for many other appointments. The children bowed and curtseyed and bid the Sun farewell until another time.

A Little Book of Mourning

Princess Hazel and Prince Phinneas looked around to see if there was any trash or sticks or pinecones to ruin the riverbanks, and threw the odd bits of leaves and bark into the river. Next, they smoothed the snow as best they could where Princess Hazel had made the first snow angel in history. Laughing, they took each other's hands and walked into the woods in search adventure.

Katherine Lench Meyering

WHAT MAKES YOU CRY THE HARDEST?
November 23, 2021

Acts of genuine kindness make me sob as if I am a two-year-old who can't find her favorite blanket.

Since August 24th, I've been washing my eyes daily with tears. They say after a catastrophic blow it's natural. My daughter died by her own hand at the age of 32. By this one act, my equilibrium and peace of mind has been blown apart.

Yet the kindness of family, friends, acquaintances and strangers has been so beautiful that it's almost sublime. The outpouring of love was, and is, staggering. The phone calls, visits, showering of flowers, cards, Facebook messages, food and gifts from all over the world swept upon us like a wave of the warmest, blue water from the Hawaiian Islands.

A Little Book of Mourning

It takes a lightening strike like this to show how much you are loved. And even in the depths of my despair, I realize that mine is a privileged grief. I'm not starving at a border of a country that doesn't want me. I live in one of my three houses. I have hot and cold running water and air conditioning and three kinds of citrus ripening on the trees in my backyard. I have the luxury of a comfortable retirement. A kind, true husband of almost 35 years. A devoted son and his family. A bouncing baby grandson. Two of the silliest pugs.

Denial, anger, bargaining, depression, acceptance. These are the stages of grief according to the Mayo Clinic website. I looked it up wanting to see if what I have been experiencing is normal. Normal. I can tell you now from experience that it is and isn't.

Katherine Lench Meyering

In the hours that followed the terrible phone call from my son-in-law, a jolt hit us. Yes, there was a feeling of numbness and shock. It was more like the feeling one gets after a car accident. Senses aware, yet everything is blurred. You lose time. I liken it to the sound that a symphonic orchestra gives. All of the sensations at once. The conductor gives the downbeat and everything assaults your ears simultaneously. Tears fall from your eyes unbidden. The heartbeat quickens. You actually do need to sit down. Breathing comes sporadically. Your head swims and you reach out.

The first few days blended into one another. And the goodwill of others began to blanket us. I called my girlfriend with the awful news. She asked me, "What can I do?" I knew I had to tell the world, but for once, didn't have any words. She sprang into action and said what needed to be said with eloquence and grace. Facebook did what it does best -- it shared.

A Little Book of Mourning

My neighbors and my Bunco gals battled over who would make us dinner each night. During the pandemic, people masked and would brave disease to visit us. We would have daily appearances of bouquets of fruit dipped in chocolate, delicacies from Zabars flown across the country, boxes of pastries, and candies. For the first days it was nearly impossible to eat, but I remember most clearly that my son made a casserole that was so delicious that we absentmindedly went back for seconds.

Flowers began pouring in with their beautiful colors, shapes, sizes and aromas filling our home. New plants would appear on our doorstep. There was a gardenia plant, an orchid that still blooms, a box of wildflower seeds, an arrangement so large that it had to be housed outside. I still read the cards that were sent, each with a message of comfort. Sometimes the cards made me cry even harder, and they all ended with the word love.

Katherine Lench Meyering

And it is that love that sustains you in the center of grief. It is each message on Facebook that is read and reread. It is each phone call made to speak about the uncomfortable truth. And so many reached out. And it was felt.

The love was like food and water and wine and honey. I have one friend who sends me a new picture of pugs every day because he knows I love them. We are on day 82. That means I have smiled at least 82 times since.

In the beginning of my anguish, I couldn't sleep. I would wake up every hour or so with my brain reeling. Images, good and bad, would flash through my mind. I remember writing to one friend trying to explain what I was going through:

> "In the aftermath of what I can only equate to being struck by lightning, we are traveling in a strange land of no sleep and

raw nerves. The only other times in my life
I felt this tired, and at the same time
tethered to 'what day or time it is?' is
actually just after giving birth. Every time
you try to fall asleep, you hear a baby cry.
But this time it's me I hear crying."

But it was music and its power of healing that
has truly touched me. Theater friends and my
song-writing collaborators sent me the gift of
music. I have been a lyricist and singer most
my life. One composer, who with me wrote a
special song for my daughter's first birthday,
sent messages of love and support. We began
writing a song to say goodbye to her. She sent
me links to Bach and came to see me and still
does. I have a girlfriend from high school who
sent me links to an orchestral medley of my
daughter's favorite film scores and her
daughter sent me the precious gift of singing,
with her ukulele, two rare songs that were my
child's signature songs.

Katherine Lench Meyering

In my twenties, I moved to New York to pursue my dreams of a life in the theater. I applied and was accepted to the BMI Musical Theater Workshop. It's a group that teaches a select group of lyricists, composers, and book writers the craft of creating musicals. If you get in, they teach you for free. In my particular class, and through my time in New York, I forged friendships that have lasted my whole life. At my darkest moments, these friends were there.

Again, the question, "What can I do?" And for them, especially, I related that I usually spent the hours of 3:00 a.m. to dawn crying. Would they please send playlists to accompany the hard times? These women and men sent me hours of music. Spotify and YouTube became a lifeline.

Two days after my daughter's death, I was wakened from an hour's nap by her voice distinctly saying, "Mom, get up. Find that lyric. You know the one. My favorite one and get it to Steve Marzullo." Steve has been my songwriting partner since 1985. He lives in New York and I in Los Angeles. In 2015, I wrote this lyric that Steve set to music, but he had never put it to paper. So, in the middle of the night, I searched my cell phone and found the lyric and the only recording of the song in existence. I sent it to him and he began to bring the song back to life. His kindness, daily phone calls full of nostalgia, politics, laughter and music are bringing me back to life.

Being a singer connects you to breathing. Breathing and making a sound is good for the soul. I have spent countless hours singing in the shower where the sound can be reverberated best -- making sounds that only I can hear. I go once a week to sing for seniors in an assisted-living home with my dear friends. We are accompanied by the amazing Ruth Allen who is a 92-year-old musical genius and her daughter who is a harmonizing gift to the world. I have been singing and healing. Writing and healing. Basking in the love of my dear friends and healing. I have spent time listening to my daughter singing. I have recordings of her singing with me that I listen to over and over again. I read the cards, messages, look at the flowers, remember the meals.

What makes you cry the hardest? Like the first note from the orchestra, it is everything all at once. Thank you. Thank you. Thank you. Happy Thanksgiving.

A Little Book of Mourning

"The Star That Shines on Me"
(lyrics by Katherine Lench Meyering, music by Steve Marzullo)

The star that shines on me
Is the star that shines on Mars.
And they tell me that this star died eons ago.

Its beams shone through the atmospheres
of galaxies still unnamed.
Its light is so bright that its death can't cover
the glow.

But I know, I know, I know
Why it shines so brightly.
I know why I know why I see it nightly.

It's the spark that makes me wake up to you
And do all the million things I'm supposed to do.
It's the thing that connects me to you.
And Mars and Saturn and Jupiter too.

Oooh

It's the thing we can't define.
It's the love that makes us shine.
I wonder if that star has us in its view.
I wonder if the star has us in its ancient view.

Katherine Lench Meyering

WHAT HAVE I BEEN DOING FOR MYSELF?

December 13, 2021

My friends have asked me what I'm doing for myself since my daughter's suicide. It's only been three and a half months since she passed. I've been going through the motions of life. I get out of bed everyday. I walk my pugs. I eat breakfast. I try to keep some sort of routine. I remind myself to drink water, to take vitamins. I visit with a few close friends when I feel strong enough. Mostly, I want to hide. I spend a lot of time prodding myself into action. I feel sleepy almost all the time. My appetite seems to have returned with a vengeance. So, I don't even get the benefit of grief-stricken weight loss. Since she left, we've had her father's birthday, Halloween, Thanksgiving, Hanukkah and my birthday. Christmas is coming and the old gray mother is getting fat.

A Little Book of Mourning

I've been going through the enormous task of preparing for Alexandra's celebration of life. We had to postpone it for a year because of the pandemic. I didn't want her sad ending to negate her many wonderful qualities. She left behind so much. She wrote seven novels. She wrote short stories, poetry and songs. Her art work adorns my home. She could be extremely funny. She connected with me almost daily. We were the kind of mother daughter combination who texted each other a great deal. I would send her funny cat things. She would send me pictures of pugs. We both reveled in a tasty recipe. We both loved naughty jokes. She was no saint, but I miss her and her neediness. I am left at sea and out of my motherly job.

I've been writing songs, essays, fragments of thought. I distract myself with listening to music, Audible books, but like tinnitus there's a high-pitched sound always ringing in my ears.

Katherine Lench Meyering

The sound keeps saying the following: I failed as a parent, mother, guardian. I have no right to offer advice or even comfort others. I missed the signs. I deserve to feel this bad.

I volunteer once a week to sing at a senior-living facility. It's my mitzvah and at times a mechaye. I recently told a friend that my rendition of "Can't Help Lovin' Dat Man" woke a few of them up! But strange things set me off crying. I am a professional singer. I have sung at funerals, wakes, and celebrations of life. People ask me, "How can you do it and not break down?" I just do.

But the other day while I was singing "What a Wonderful World," I could barely breathe. I certainly couldn't continue singing and I thought I'd have to run sobbing from the room. Luckily, my audience couldn't see or hear very well, and for that matter, didn't notice. And as luck would have it, I wasn't singing alone. I summoned my years of technique and breathing exercises and finished the song. There was something about the lyric about babies crying that got to me.

When will I stop doing emotional needlepoint on my heart? As it's the second week of December, we changed the song program at the old folks' home. Now we're singing Christmas songs. These songs are already loaded with emotional baggage like the ghosts of Christmas past and present. Even for the hard of hearing, a single refrain of "I'll Be Home for Christmas" can start the waterworks in the entire room. But I do know from personal experience that a good cry is good for the soul. By now, my soul should be shining.

I wonder if my house is haunted? Maybe. When I was a little girl, I used to have the occasional nightmare. I would run to my mother and father. I think it was my mother who explained that your waking life is like the carousel on a slide projector. The things you see are placed before you in a logical order.

And that the Operator of the projector showed them to you in the perfect way. But when you're dreaming, the Operator goes home to bed, leaving the slide projector to show any random thing it wants. And if I was having a bad dream, all I had to do was wake up and tell the Operator to come back and show me things in the correct order. That made sense to me back then. It helped me to control my bad dreams. Whenever things got intense, I would mentally wake up and ask the Operator to go back to work.

Recently, though, my Operator has gone on a permanent vacation. Whether I'm waking or sleeping, slides of my past life, future life, scenes from holidays, trips, and seemingly meaningless events pop into my vision unbidden. I can walk into my daughter's room and see her at age four sleeping in her bed, at age ten reading, at age 18 getting ready for a date, at age 25 trying on her wedding dress, at age 32 settling into sleep with our pug, Vinny, all at the same time. I hear her voice saying her catch phrases. Just before I go to sleep, I envisage her final moments and ask myself if she was scared, determined, drunk, crazed, in pain, at peace?

I keep trying to make sense of something that makes no sense. I don't understand. And yet I do. The actress in me can pretend to be in her shoes. I have an abundance of empathy. If I see someone with a cut or bruise, I actually feel pain in my body. If I see someone crying, I start to cry, too. I feel her pain every day. And I feel a worse pain knowing that I could do nothing to take that pain away.

If heaven and hell are all here on earth simultaneously, then I am in both. I love some of my memories of her. I remember how truly beautiful she was. She had the perfect nose. Of all of our family, with different shaped noses, hers was the most beautifully defined. Her long brown hair was a sight to behold. Her face could be warm and expressive. Her laugh was literally contagious. Her wit, sense of humor, and moral compass were enviable. I always imagined her to be reincarnated from one of those suffragettes who chained themselves to things in righteous protest. She was a defender of the weak and outcast.

My heaven is in these remembrances. My hell is her existence wiped away in a violent act. And sadly, for now, it is the violent act that won't leave my mind. I have been calling for my Operator to take that slide and burn it. But he is on vacation and the slide keeps showing up. And yet, if I'm very good and get up every day and go through the motions of life, I get a fleeting glimpse of her smile right before I wake up. There she is, just around that corner of my mind. There she is.

A Little Book of Mourning

Katherine Lench Meyering

I JOINED A CLUB. MERRY CHRISTMAS

December 2021

I joined a club I never wanted admittance to. I never in a million years thought I'd be one of those parents.

Once, on a cruise to Mexico, David, the quirky member of the entertainment staff who was from England, told me I reminded him of Amy Winehouse's mum. She was a friend of his mother's, and he said I was so like her in looks and demeanor that it took him aback. I didn't know how to receive that information. My daughter was with us then with her husband and our son. This was our first night on board and we had all sung karaoke. My daughter belted out "Bad Romance" by Lady Gaga. She was wonderful, dressed in a little black dress, with her long hair flowing as she sang. We were all together and happy and looking forward to the voyage.

A Little Book of Mourning

We kept seeing David all over the ship: at Bingo, Trivia contests, Holiday celebrations -- even a quickly pulled-together set of candle-lighting parties for the eight nights of Hanukkah.

David was a funny, original fellow who was working on his first cruise for this line of ships. His droll sense of humor and strange vocal resemblance to Ronald Coleman struck us as funny, and we remember some of the witty things he said to this day. We use them as family quotes. We knew him for a week but he made a lasting impression on us all. My daughter, in particular, loved him. She always joked that she wished our son was gay so David could become my other son-in-law. I agreed. But my son wasn't on board with that.

In a way, my daughter was more like Amy Winehouse than we knew. Only my girl wasn't famous…yet.

Katherine Lench Meyering

Like Amy, she was talented, beautiful, tortured, driven, and magnificent. Like Amy, she was a sufferer of profound depression and had issues with alcohol and drugs. Like Amy, she burnt like a comet. Like Amy, it seems, none of the psychiatrists or anti-depressants seemed to help. Like Amy, nothing was going to keep her from her date with suicide.

In the wake of my daughter's death, we have learned many things we didn't know about how severe her struggles were and about the timeline that led up to her final moments. If I had known some of this before the event, I might have been more vigilant. If I had explored her Instagram account in 2017, I would have seen a piece of art she had done depicting her face of depression with an inner monologue of self hate and disparagement. What struck me most when I saw it, was how much the woman in the center looks like me, my grandmother and my daughter. It chilled my heart and continues to do so.

A Little Book of Mourning

But I never paid attention to Instagram. I'm old. If I had seen it then, I think I would have taken her more seriously. I like to think I would have gone to therapy with her. But she was a master at hiding it. She would talk and say she was depressed, but because I didn't have her delusional brain, I couldn't understand what it was like for her. When I get depressed, I get down on my hands and knees and wash my kitchen floor. And I feel better. When I get depressed, I write a poem or listen to music, or eat chocolate. And I feel better.

My daughter was so good at expressing herself artistically. She was a writer, singer, pianist, a fine artist. She was a student of philosophy. At the time of her death, she had just completed her master's degree and was about to enter a five-year program to receive her PhD.

But back in 2017 on our cruise to Mexico, we had no idea what was to come, and were in high spirits and having a wonderful time. My daughter was at her best on a holiday. And Christmas was coming. The ship was trimmed with holiday trees and tinsel and fake snow and sparkle. She loved fine dining, cocktails, coffee, dressing up. She adored exploring the ship and sleeping late and she and her husband were so in love. The ship was aglow with pre-Christmas cheer and the wonderful Mariachi band, Los Brillantes, was playing "Feliz Navidad."

I remember the days full of hot December sunshine as we pulled into various ports. I remember every night dining at our reserved table with our devoted Filipino waiter, Elmer. He got such a kick out of my daughter who kept ordering shrimp cocktails. Eventually, Elmer would bring her three at a time and laughed along with us enjoying her delight! My girl would laugh so hard during those evenings that she'd have to lay her head on the table, tears running down her face. People at other tables would watch us collapsing with laughter and smile, yearning to know what was so funny.

Katherine Lench Meyering

Back then, her world was full of possibilities. She was newly married, back from Japan where she'd taught English to Japanese children. Even then, she struggled with anxiety, but on this trip she seemed better. She'd already finished writing and self-publishing four novels.

Little did she know that she'd finally have a new one published legitimately.

Her father and I secretly hoped that these two newlyweds would have a baby we could love and adore. That child would have been beautiful to look at and have our daughter's brilliance and her husband's sweet nature.

But this year, Thanksgiving is approaching then Hanukkah and inevitably Christmas. This year, I won't celebrate any of them. This year I remember David, the assistant cruise entertainment director, and how funny he was and how nice he was to my daughter and how

A Little Book of Mourning

she loved him after such a brief encounter. I remember the waiter, Elmer, who delivered never ending shrimp cocktails.

This year, the ink is drying on my membership card to the club I never wanted to join. I can't control which images of a life lived and lost pop into my weary mind.

I won't even wonder why I sob embarrassingly through "Feliz Navidad."

Yes, I've joined the club where you never stop asking why. I wonder how Amy Winehouse's mum is feeling? What it was like for her? Am I really like her? In many ways, I must be.

And as another warmish California Christmas is lurking, I am reminded of our cruise to Mexico. And I feel the breezes all around me as I glide through the Mexican waters of my memory. It is a melancholy trip but in a strange way it's uplifting and dare I say, enlightening?

But for God's sake, please don't play "Have Yourself a Merry Little Christmas."

ঙ৺ঙ

WOMB TO TOMB

January 12, 2022

When I was 20, I was in a production of *West Side Story*. I played one of the Shark girlfriends and got to sing the song "Somewhere" from the orchestra pit during a dreamy ballet featuring Tony and Maria. The line, "Womb to tomb," spoken by Riff and Tony in the prelude to the "Jet Song," is taking on a new meaning for me these days. My daughter was born on August 11, 1989. She died by her own hand on August 24, 2021. I never in a million years thought I would be there for her last day on earth. In the natural order, I would go before her. But, from her inception to her demise, she always did things in her own way.

My husband and I got together later than most couples of our generation. I had been an actress pursing my dreams of Broadway and fame. He was also a stage actor who had, by chance and hard work, forged a career in television, film, and writing. He was by far the more successful of the two of us. I was 30 when we married. He was 35. It seemed logical that we would start our family sooner than later and only had two years of married life without children.

I had had a history of painful endometriosis, and thought it would be difficult for me to conceive a child. But as fate would have it, two weeks of trying resulted in a pregnancy! The night I took the test, I was wakened by an earthquake. It was near three in the morning and the jolt woke me. I walked queasily to the bathroom and, when I emerged, I knew we were going to be parents.

A little more than nine months later, near midnight, my water broke and we drove over the hill from the San Fernando Valley onto Sunset Boulevard heading to Cedars-Sinai Hospital. I remember we were following a pickup truck with two teenage girls riding in the back. They seemed to be having a wonderful time in the open air of a hot August night. I think we remarked that we would never let our girl ride in an open pickup bed at midnight. We were going to be good parents!

Thirty-four hours later, after a very difficult back labor and an eventual C-section, our daughter was born. She had been facing the wrong way, and in the emergency surgery the doctor had nicked her cheek with the scalpel. We counted ourselves lucky that the scalpel hadn't hit her eye. The night she was born coincided with the Perseid meteor shower. We knew she was going to be remarkable.

After the exhausting birth, we took our angel home and she proceeded to cry for three months. She had the worst colic. She would begin wailing at 3:00 p.m. and wouldn't stop until 5:00 or 6:00 a.m. We were distraught.

Katherine Lench Meyering

The only thing that would soothe her was to drive at exactly 55 miles per hour. Any faster or slower would bring on the screeching. We were so desperate one night we dialed 1-800-NOCOLIC. For lots of money they send you a machine that you can attach to the crib to shake it and play white noise. It simulates a car ride. We were warned by the instructions not to let the machine run for more than an hour.

After three months, it brought relief. One night, we were surprised at how long we all had slept. Then with a rush to the room, we realized that the machine had been on for three hours. There, sleeping peacefully, in a shaky crib, was our baby. What had we done? Had we addled her? We were going to be good parents. Had we failed? The baby awoke refreshed and didn't seem any worse for her longer-than-normal simulated ride to Pasadena and back!

A Little Book of Mourning

Many times a day, I wander back to her childhood, combing my memory for clues. Was it the time I made her sit still as I cut her bangs? Was it the time I insisted she use the potty? Was it the day I dropped her off at kindergarten when she was crying and I walked away? Was it my stern voice trying to discipline her? What had I done in trying to tame her wild, defiant nature into an acceptable child who ate with a knife and fork and said please and thank you that I could have done differently?

As a child, my daughter had an extremely strong will. She was, in my opinion, overly sensitive about weird things. She took a strong aversion to certain colors. It would send her into a fit if her socks were on correctly and she could feel the "bumps" in the fabric that connected them. She wouldn't stick to a bed time and had trouble sleeping. She was prone to nightmares. She would cuddle only when we read to her, and didn't like to be touched at any other time. She refused all attempts to teach her to clean or get her room in order. My mother assured me that all children were like that and she would grow out of it. She didn't.

But even with her extremes, she could also be sweet. She was fiercely intelligent, creative and full of wonder. Each childhood milestone, from rolling over to walking, to speaking, to teething, came early. She had a great sense of humor. She could run before she knew what she was doing. It was a challenge to keep her from hurting herself.

After her little brother was born, she was naturally jealous, but learned to love him. The two soon became inseparable. We noticed shortly after my son's birth that what we thought was my daughter's lazy eye turned out to be much more serious.

A Little Book of Mourning

She had strabismus (classic crossed eyes) and was in danger of losing her eyesight. We were sent to a specialist who had us start patching her weak eye and prescribed thick glasses. Thus began a battle to keep her from losing, scratching, or dismantling her glasses. The patching was difficult and painful for her. She often had to be held down to put the patch on. She couldn't understand why we were doing this to her. We were saving her eyesight, but it was my little girl who was in pain and frustrated.

Eventually she had a surgery when she was nine years old which helped correct and preserve her vision. The surgery was traumatic for her and for us. The surgeon said if his own child had the same eyesight issues, he would have the surgery done in a heartbeat. To this day, I feel we made the right decision for our child. But I often wonder if that early trauma contributed to her woes as an adult.

Katherine Lench Meyering

When she was old enough to notice, she found the scar on her cheek about an inch beneath her eye. "Why do I have this?" She asked. I told her that she was like a Ming vase with one tiny flaw. Nearly perfect. I told her that it was from her emergency birth and even though she was hurt, she was alive.

I am looking for a reason for my daughter's suicide. I am looking hard at myself to see if I am to blame. I am trying to dissect her life to find out what influenced her to take such a drastic step. I am also aware that it isn't one thing that could have caused it, but an accumulation of experiences and her natural genetic "wiring" that contributed to her deep depression. She was so like my mother. They shared the same brilliance and with that brilliance came a need in both of them to self-medicate. She was so like my father in her love and facility for language. With his strong sense of right and wrong. He, too, drank a great deal.

A Little Book of Mourning

My family has a history of alcoholism. I like to drink, but luckily because of a weak stomach, can't overly indulge. One of my favorite quotes has been, "Do you drink? Not as much as I'd like to."

But my daughter could outdrink us all. Combined with her lifelong insomnia and use of prescription sleep medicine, she was slowly destroying her existence. It saddens me deeply that toward the end of her life her corrected eye was loosening. She was told by her optometrist that she would most likely need another surgery to keep her eyes from re-crossing. She told me that she was losing sight in one eye. She also mentioned that she was having to patch the weak eye in preparation for that surgery. She confided that she found the patching exhausting. She also had some pending dental work that had to be attended to before she was to leave town. She had been accepted to the PhD program at UC

Santa Cruz and was about to begin her studies in a few weeks.

There were many things I didn't know about her medical treatment. She was under the care of a psychiatrist. I was aware that many of the anti-depressants she took were not effective. I tried many times to reason with her that if she drank alcohol, it would negate the other drugs she took. She would assure me she was okay.

My daughter was an adult of 32. She was working with her doctors to combat her depression. She was trying hard to fight it. She eventually turned to the experimental treatment of ketamine. She assured us it was supervised and it had been reported to have amazing effects. She believed it was possible to have her depression wiped away with as little as two treatments. It was not covered by insurance. She was going to do it. I think she was desperate for an instant cure.

A Little Book of Mourning

After the treatment, she told us that although it was thoroughly unpleasant, it had lifted the fog she was under. She genuinely felt better. She said she found it profoundly disturbing to have the complete out-of-body experience the drug induced and canceled the next treatment scheduled for later in the month. She said that in order to take the next treatment, she'd have to stop drinking and she didn't want to do that.

And to us, she did seem better. She was busy making plans for her new apartment in Santa Cruz. We celebrated her birthday with a dinner out at a nice restaurant. She asked to borrow our house and threw a party for about 30 of her friends. She went to great pains to provide special birthday cakes for each of the four guests (herself included) who had August birthdays.

We were planning a trip to her favorite vacation spot which was on the way to Santa

Cruz. She cooked me a delicious Japanese meal and I spent the evening, together with her husband, singing karaoke and watching a new animated movie. The last thing she said to me was, "Text me the minute you get home. You know how I worry about you!" I lived about three minutes from her house.

Four days later she would be dead.

She was a writer and a philosophy student. We shared a love of the written word. I proofread everything she wrote. Her last written word to me was, "Heyy."

When we first knew of her existence, there was an earthquake. When she was born, meteors fell from the sky. When she died, the earthquakes and meteors of life broke my Ming vase. And broke me too.

We were going to be good parents.

A Little Book of Mourning

ೊ
TO MY MOTHER, FOR HER STRENGTH
March 8, 2022

The six-month anniversary of my daughter's suicide has come and gone. I am surprised that I haven't felt impelled to write about its commemoration before now. Writing has been my salvation living in this no man's land of grief. My writing has bordered on compulsion. I think it's a way of keeping me distracted from dealing with the deepest hurt that I've locked away. I have had to steel my inner weaknesses to continue the day to day of living. My dogs need walks and to be fed. My husband and I have our routines that keep us amongst the living. The trash needs to be taken out, meals must be cooked, beds are made and undone and remade. Someone should wash the kitchen floor…maybe I'll do it today.

There are things I have left undone for way too long and they are starting to find their way into my consciousness. When my daughter was alive, I began crocheting a soft, thick, gray blanket. I am three quarters of the way done and I can't for the life of me pick it up and finish it. I wasn't sure if I was going to keep it for myself or give it to her. Now it's been so long that I can't even remember the simple pattern. Every day, it sits in my closet daring me to begin again. Every morning, I say maybe I'll do it today.

Due to the pandemic and my natural inclination to put things off, I haven't made

A Little Book of Mourning

an appointment to have my teeth cleaned. I could be vacuuming my house. I could do so many things, but just don't have the energy or interest. I am inert.

Some of things I have done:

1. Helped my husband plant spring flowers.
2. Finally had my yearly (after two years) physical.
3. Started a diet.
4. Due to a medication, stopped drinking (6 weeks).
5. Babysat for my grandson.

Like the "good girl, A-student" I always was, I tell myself that by completing these tasks I will achieve my goal and make progress. Toward what? Another goal? A clearer mind? A rest from the overwhelming grief? A sense of normalcy.

I know that this is naive. But there's a part of me that is sure that I can't sustain the level of sadness that envelops me and continue to live what I suspect may be a long life. So, I am fighting the urge to completely give up.

Katherine Lench Meyering

And then there's the window. I have all the windows from my Idaho house which was built in 1928. My mother was born the next year. We had the windows replaced and I couldn't bear to throw these original weather-beaten antiques away. I made my husband drag them back to my other home in California where they sit in a shed waiting for me to turn them into art.

But my daughter was the real artist. I gave her one of the windows and bought her paint that is perfect for painting glass. She was in the process of painting a three-paned window with illustrations from her last novel *The King of Verdance*. *Verdance* is a fantasy book that takes place in the desert, the Kingdom of Verdance and in the sky. It has a hot-air balloon and many wondrous steampunky things born from her vast imagination.

She completed one of the panels and was in the middle of the second when she died. She left sketches of what the other two panels should look like. I am enough of an artist that

Katherine Lench Meyering

I could complete this piece of art. But it's hers, not mine. And like her, it is incomplete. I keep meaning to get out the paints and attempt it. But like the half-done blanket, I'm finding it impossible to begin.

Her artistry was a matter of pride for our whole family. We used to brag that she was a Renaissance Woman. She was fluent in Japanese, a fine artist, a novelist, a lyricist, a composer. She played the piano, flute, ukulele, ocarina, and banjo. She earned a master's degree in philosophy and was about to begin classes for her PhD in it. She was a champion of the small and weak. She was an advocate for the underdog. She loved our pugs, Vinny and Zuul, so much that she immortalized them in *The King of Verdance* as the characters Francois and Etienne.

So, how can any of us hope to finish what she began? The unfinished window may have to stay unfinished. My unfinished blanket may never be complete. My still-broken heart may have to wait a very long time to mend. I have to acknowledge that life, as I knew it, will never be the same.

A Little Book of Mourning

As I inch toward feeling better, I am reminded of my daughter when she was a small baby burdened with a fierce colic. She would try to crawl away from the pain in her tummy, searching for a place where she could relax. Like her, I am trying to crawl away from my pain. We all are.

I have a friend who lost her best friend to cancer. It is so hard for her to come to terms with her friend's death that she is still reeling from the pain. I have another friend whose mother passed not long ago. He is dealing with the profound loss. Their pain is my pain. I understand them and grieve with them.

My husband and son are processing my daughter's death in very different ways from mine. It is heartbreaking for me to see others hurting. If I see someone cut or bleeding, I tend to get dizzy and faint. To live with this coat of sadness that my family and close friends are wearing now is almost more than I can stand.

But as each day dawns, I try.

Katherine Lench Meyering

I am also fully aware that the day-to-day assault from the pandemic, the unspeakable war in Ukraine, and our exhausting political climate take a great toll on all of us collectively. And my heart's energy doesn't want to exclude my soul into neglecting the world at large.

But in my smaller world, I walk the dogs. I cook the meals. I continue writing, singing, breathing. I can't think that my dearly departed daughter would want it any other way. I just can't let this defeat me. I realize that I am not alone.

My daughter wrote a novella called *The Hunter's Bond* and on the inscription page she wrote:

To my mother,

for her strength

This has become my new mantra. I say it to myself every morning. I say it to myself every night. And sometimes I believe it.

A Little Book of Mourning

HOLIDAYS ARE HARD

July 12, 2023

It'll be two years since my daughter took her life on August 24th. Our family has gone through all the stages of grief -- sometimes all at the same time. Sometimes denial is my strongest reaction to her death. I still think my daughter is living an alternative life in Japan. Sometimes I think she is completing her second year of grad school at UC Santa Cruz -- exploring philosophy -- or that she is completing the trilogy of novels she began about the fantastic events in Verdance, a kingdom she invented. I yearn to believe she's on a retreat somewhere perfecting her artwork, or writing new songs, or playing the piano or drinking cocktails or roaming around Cambria, collecting stones on Moonstone Beach.

Katherine Lench Meyering

I hear her voice often. She had a few catch phrases that we all have adopted. One of my favorite phrases was about our pug, Vinny. With a big smile and a wink, she'd say, "He's not that good!" She was right about that. Most often I hear her say, "That's okay!" She said it in a kind of sing-song way that charmed me when she was a child…and continued to soothe me when she left us at age 32.

She loved holidays. She really loved the Fourth of July. For the last two years, we have kept celebrating anything to a minimum. My husband and I, don't have the strength or desire to make the effort.

Our son lives nearby and feels his sister's loss in a different way. But life has to go on. He has an eight-year-old stepson and our grandchild is almost three. It was time this year to put on a Fourth of July party. I felt strongly that it would be good for the kids to see our house decorated and to throw a BBQ.

So, I carry on and there are moments when I enjoy things again. I tell myself I'm doing it for her. I planted sunflowers, her favorite flower, in the garden we created in her memory. They have grown so tall. It's a forest ablaze with yellow, black and brown and lots of green. The stalks reach up almost to heaven (or Nirvana or Valhalla, or Never Neverland or the Shire or the bee-loud glade or wherever she is) and grace the sky with their height and splendor. I talk to the palo verde tree we planted in the garden, now covered with tiny yellow flowers. I welcome the bees. I once wrote a song about freesias.

I found religion in a flow'r. Deep purple fused with gold...

Yesterday, I filched a few freesia bulbs from the front yard and planted them next to the sign that says "Al's Garden." On the sign is her favorite poem by Yeats.

She had so many talents and wrote songs so easily. I often struggle with each word of my lyrics, but hers flowed out of her seemingly without effort. She wrote about the Fourth of July in her song "Lost Among the Waves:"

...and I'll think of you watching fireworks on
*   the Fourth of July.*
I'm still grasping at the memory of your
*   last sweet lullaby.*
And I'm still here screaming and begging
*   the reason why?*
Can you hear me? Can you hear me?
Whispering goodbye.
And I still expect to find you when
*   the dawn turns to day*
As I break beneath the burden of the crimes
*   that you forgave.*
And I'm still here waiting beside the arbor grave.
For the moment. For the moment of
*   the quieting of waves.*

A Little Book of Mourning

I keep asking myself, was she prescient or just a very good writer? How did she know how I'd feel in the aftermath of her demise. She was an old soul. She was wise and caring and brilliant and expressive. She loved words and poetry and mythology and me.

And with all my book learning and literacy and wordsmithing, I can't for the life of me figure out how I missed the signs. How I kept my eye off the ball and let this miracle slip away.

And I'm still here waiting for the quieting of waves, and sometimes if I listen very carefully, I can hear her say, "That's okay!"

Katherine Lench Meyering

A Little Book of Mourning

◈◈◈

THE NIGHT BEFORE THAT FATEFUL DAY

August 23, 2024

Tomorrow is the third anniversary of the worst thing that has ever happened to me.

My beautiful daughter snuffed out her own life on August 24th, 2021. And this morning my husband had to remind me that tomorrow is once again the resurrection of that awful day.

To be fair, I've been sick for the last two weeks with a cough that has turned into a kind of asthma. My cough has been incessant and I've been sleep-deprived and incredibly self-involved. I've spent this last year distracting myself. I've listened to 88 novels. I've listened to lots and lots of music. I've sung for the elderly. I've sung in my shower. I've walked miles and miles as the rhythm of my heart and sound of my steps separates me from the deep pain.

My husband wrote a profound and beautiful play that deals directly and indirectly about our experiences -- about the aftermath.

We survived. We rode the roller coaster and though I wanted desperately to get off that ride; I screamed and cried and wrote and worried and carried on and sucked it up and continued to live.

So how could I have forgotten?

But as the day progressed, images forced their way to my consciousness: baby Alex sitting in my lap by my parent's swimming pool, Alex wearing a birthday hat -- surrounded by balloons, Alex dressed in a pink harem costume wearing her cherry red Mickey Mouse glasses for Halloween, Alex riding a pony, Alex swimming with her brother, Alex, at about eight years old, cooking in our

A Little Book of Mourning

kitchen in Santa Clarita, dressed in a blue dress wearing earrings, Alex at the piano, Alex laughing, Alex at her prom, Alex drinking wine, Alex in her wedding dress, Alex accepting her awards, her diplomas, her applause, Alex surrounded by her friends, family, husband. There are so many images. And while I was remembering and unwrapping the images that burn but also bring joy, I thought this must be for me as it is for many.

What I've been going through has now become a kind of aversion therapy. How many times can I look at an image and not cry? How many times can I tell a funny story and not cry. How many times can I reveal that I'm still furious that my dear, dear daughter won't be here to enjoy that party or drink more wine or tell us a new funny story or share in a glorious moment or pet our dogs or watch her nephew grow up or see me go gray.

Katherine Lench Meyering

Last year I had a productive year. This year I've had a distracted year.

She left me to it. And it's not fair. I waited up till midnight. I wanted to remember that three years ago, on this night, she was still alive.

∼⋄∽

August 24, 2024

And today is here. And I'm dry-eyed. The morning is fresh. Her commemorative tree is green and growing. The dogs are here wanting breakfast. I'll walk two miles today and get a decaf coffee.

Life is still going on. I will honor Alex. I will say her name and try and thank her for the gifts she gave. Today is not a day for anger, or denial, or despair. It is a day of acceptance. Today is day of remembrance. I will see the light and air and hear the music and love the flowers and bees and I will hope and carry on with love and joy.

A Little Book of Mourning

෴
AFTERWARD
September 17, 2024

As I come to the close of my little book of mourning, I can honesty say that although the past three years have been difficult, heartbreaking and, at times, unbearable, I have come to look at this journey as a gift. The grief unlocked a well of creativity in me. I hope I've become a better person. I certainly don't take things for granted. I am lucky to be alive and lucky to have known Alex. She helped me grow.

This is the lyric I wrote for her first birthday. Marjorie wrote beautiful music for it.

Who's behind those eyes so perfect
    and so new?
You're just a year on Saturday.
I can't believe it's true.

Who's behind that smile -- that burst of
sunshine there?
Are you that glad to look at me?
Forgive me if I stare.

Ally,
Ally
I'm glad that you chose me.
There's such a lot of world out there.
Such a lot to be.

A Little Book of Mourning

Who's behind that door? Who's waiting to
come through?
My one-year-old.
My miracle.
My baby girl, that's who.

Katherine Lench Meyering

A Little Book of Mourning

"That's okay."

Alexandra Mitsch Meyering

THANKS TO

The Fellowship:

Ralph Meyering, Jr.
Max Meyering and family
Chris Mitsch
Jeff Mitsch
Sandy Mitsch
Eric Mitsch
Camille S. Thien
Marjorie Poe
Steve Marzullo
Ron Rocha
Barbara Baer
Ruth Allen
Beth Halpin
Charles Garside
Gail Garside
Bradley Land
Margaret Pine
Lynn Ahrens
Laura Pavey
Hayley Grenrock
Laura Gleason
Michele Buttleman
Charles Herrera
Catherine Fries Vaughn
Fiama Fricano Traxler
Andrea Randall
Lynsey Carman
Margo Whitby
Sally Wilfert
Steve Hammer
Claire Rydell
Core Four
The Bunco Gals
And many, many others
who took the time and walked with me
and listened when it was not fun.

NOTES

Katherine Lench Meyering is a singer, actress, lyricist, and voice teacher. She lives in Santa Clarita, California and Coeur d'Alene Idaho. Her voice can be heard singing and speaking daily in many Disney theme parks. She is married to actor/writer Ralph Meyering, Jr. and lives with two elderly pugs, Vinny and Zuul.

Books by Alex:

THE RESURRECTIONIST

In 19th century Scotland, surgeon Edgar Price has only days to live. He has become host to a revenant that will corrode both his body and soul. Edgar's fatal mistake has not only doomed him, but also released six more of these malignant wraiths onto the world. In his remaining time, he has vowed to stop the revenants from claiming other victims. His perilous travels lead him to the Witches' Wood, a haven for a sisterhood of powerful enchantresses. There he meets Ainsley, a witch with a fiery spirit and strong distrust of outsiders. She too is racing against the clock to save her life and will go to any lengths to spare her lover Colleen from the grief of losing her. Despite their mutual dislike, Edgar and Ainsley find that the only way to traverse the twisted, otherworldly labyrinths that the revenants have created is to work together. Their mission becomes further complicated when Edgar begins to develop strong feelings for Fana, the guardian goddess of the Wood, in spite of Ainsley's forbidding warnings to stay far away from her.

Horror and fantasy intermingle in this imagined continuation to the true story of the Burke and Hare murders

THE HUNTER'S BOND:
A TALE OF THE DAWN MIRROR CHRONICLES

A storybook life ended in one bloody night...

Left injured, alone, and penniless, noblewoman Beatrice Langford can only think of exacting revenge on the ones who took everything from her. After getting a job as a barmaid from tavern-owner Miles Creedy, she soon discovers his dark secret. Following Creedy into the underworld of crime and vigilante punishment, she is tempted by an opportunity to learn skills deadly enough to carry out her vengeful plan. Beatrice may need to sacrifice everything in order to succeed, including her humanity.

EDEN UNDONE:
THE DAWN MIRROR CHRONICLES BOOK 2

The girl who conquered an Angel rises again. The Angel Nestor is gone, a mysterious stranger lurks in the shadows, and Penny Fairfax has tempted the Cardinal's ire. The adventures continue in the second volume of Dawn Mirror Chronicles, Eden Undone.

A war is brewing in Elydria. In the months since Penny thwarted the Angel Nestor's barbaric plans, turbulent times have been raging throughout Elydria. As Penny deals with the aftermath, a gruesome catastrophe rocks Iverton. The Cardinal threatens a political coup by the Order of Nestor if the Angel isn't soon found.

THE ANGEL OF ELYDRIA
BOOK ONE OF THE DAWN MIRROR CHRONICLES

At the crossroads where dreams become nightmares lies the world of Elydria...

It's not every day that a college student dies and is revived in a distant world far away from her small hometown in Oregon. But that's exactly what happens to Penny Fairfax. Penny soon discovers her near death experience awakened an ability to manipulate the dreams of others, permitting her to unlock hidden secrets from the past and create vivid illusions.

Trapped in Elydria with her English professor, Penny must navigate a world of gas lamps and glittering façades on the verge of collapse in search of the way home. Haunted by a malicious specter wearing an iron funeral mask, she learns that her gift of life comes with a high cost. Now, Penny must escape its wicked intentions, solve the mystery that is unleashing havoc on Elydria, and return home without meeting death a second time.

UNREAL CITY

Sarah Wilkes is desperate enough to do anything, even make a deal with the devil - or in her case, a familiar spirit. After her twin Lea is murdered, Sarah finds college life impossible and longs to escape. Everything changes when Sarah realizes a familiar spirit is stalking her and offers to transport her to the terrifying and fantastical realm of Unreal City. The payment for admission? A taste of her blood. Unable to resist, Sarah is drawn into an alternate reality that is a dream come true... at first.

The deeper she explores Unreal City, the more Sarah's reality becomes warped. Death surrounds her as people are murdered in the same fashion as her sister. She has no choice but to continue her visits to Unreal City, which grows darker by the day. Is finding out the truth about what happened to Lea worth becoming part of Unreal City forever?

www.ingramcontent.com/pod-product-compliance
Lightning Source LLC
Chambersburg PA
CBHW060817050426
42449CB00008B/1697